Author: Laurel Reuter
Editor: Matthew Koumis
Translation: Kaeko Nakagawa;
and META4
Sub-Editor: Mary-Rose Tatham
Graphic Design: Rachael Dadd
Reprographics: Ermanno Beverari
Printed in Italy by Grafiche AZ

Telos Art Publishing
PO Box 125, Winchester
SO23 7UJ England
t: +44 (0) 1962 864546
f: +44 (0) 1962 864727
e: editorial@telos.net
e: sales@telos.net
w: www.arttextiles.com

ISBN 1 902015 59 2 (softback)
ISBN 1 902015 60 6 (hardback)

A CIP catalogue record for this book
is available from The British Library

Notes
All dimensions are shown in metric
and imperial, height x width [x depth].

Photo Credits
Takashi Hatakeyama, Sendai Photo
Studio, Hiroshi Kimura, Naoto Hasegawa,
Philip Carr, Akira Koike, Rik Sferra

Publisher's Acknowledgements
With thanks to Laurel, to Erin Prues,
Kristina Detwiller, Freya, John Denison,
Sue Atkinson, Giorgio and Stefania,
Simone and to the whole team in Verona.

Illustrations:
front cover
Untitled
2001
fishing line, stainless wire, kozo
13 x 19 x 48ft (4 x 6 x 15m)

back cover
Untitled (detail)
1995
pulp, kozo, soil, sisal, bamboo, manila
hemp, expanded polystyrene
fourteen pieces, overall dimensions:
4 x 13 x 8in (110 x 35 x 20cm)

pages 1 & 48
Untitled (detail)
fishing line, knitting
600 x 700 x 50cm

portfolio collection
Machiko Agano

TELOS

Contents

Untitled
1989
pulp, soil, sisal, expanded polystyrene
12 x 35 x 85in (30 x 90 x 220cm)

Foreword

2001年4月28日から6月24日までイギリス東南部のサリー、ロチェスター、ブライトンの3市で同時に「テクスチュラル　スペース (素材空間) ― 現代日本のテクスタイル・アート」展が開かれ、人々から好評を持って迎えられたと聞く。ブライトンでは、ブライトン・フェスティバルの一環として開かれたためもあって、多くの観客を集めたが、なかでも上野真知子の作品が大いに話題を呼んだという。

ブライトンでは美術館とファブリカギャラリーの2会場で開催されたが、上野の個展に与えられたのは、もと教会だったファブリカギャラリーであった。彼女は空間がもつ一種神秘的な雰囲気を感じ取り、それに呼応する神秘的な力を表明する作品を創ることを意図したのである。

上野の作品は透明なナイロン糸とステンレスワイヤーを一組の編棒で、幅6メートル、長さ約40メートルに編み上げ、そのつなぎ目のない一枚の網を天井から吊り、また床に固定して、あたかも大海の波のような起伏を造り、それに印象的な効果を与える為に、部分的に楮をかけ、照明したものである。まさに豊かな深さと広がりを有する神秘的な空間がうまれたであろうことが想像できる。

さらにまたギャラリーの空間そのものも普段の表情とは一変して、一種荘厳な雰囲気を漂わせていたに違いない。イギリスの人々はこれまで知らなかった糸による造形と、それが発する静かなしかし力強い響きに魅了されたのであろう。会場に充満する静やかで、清らかな気に人々は浸った。ギャラリーは入場を制限しなければならないほどの入りだったという。

In three towns in the South East of England – Surrey, Rochester and Brighton, the exhibition "Textural Space: Contemporary Japanese textile art" was held simultaneously from 28 April to 24 June 2001. It drew many visitors in Brighton, partly because it was held as part of the Brighton Festival. The exhibition seems to have been favourably received and the work of Machiko Agano is said to have been the focus of most attention.

In Brighton, the exhibition was held at two locations – the Museum and the Fabrica Gallery. Agano's exhibit was at the Fabrica, which used to be a church. In response to the atmosphere of the space she created works that would express its mystery.

Agano's creations, six metres wide and about 40 metres long, made from translucent nylon thread and stainless steel wire, are knitted using a single set of knitting needles. These seamless mesh sheets are hung from the ceiling and fixed to the floor, forming waves reminiscent of the ocean, partially hung and illuminated to give a powerful impression. The space took on a mystical quality born out of the open skies of Agano's creative spirit.

The gallery itself must have had a kind of dignity, something different from its usual atmosphere. The British audience was spellbound by Agano's thread creations, by their originality and their tranquillity. The form seems to stimulate the imagination creating echoes in the mind of a receptive audience.

The atmosphere of quiet and purity that permeated the place attracted large numbers. It was so popular that admission had to be limited.

Untitled
2001
fishing line, stainless wire, kozo
13 x 19 x 48ft (4 x 6 x 15m)
commissioned by Brighton Festival,
Surrey Institute

above:
Untitled (detail)
1997
fishing line, stainless wire
13 x 19 x 26ft (4 x 6 x 8m)

right:
Untitled
1996
installation
fishing line, stainless wire

京都市立芸術大学では、伝統的な織を学んだ上野真知子は1980年代の初めから、薄く透き通ったシルクオーガンジーの布を用いたインスタレーション的作品を発表するようになり、そうした作品でスイス・ローザンヌ国際タピスリービエンナーレにも選ばれて出品している。1992年の同ビエンナーレでは、会場エントランスの空間を与えられ、ジグザグに折り曲がりながら流れるようにたれる多数の布によって3層吹き抜けの大きな空間を埋め、布を通りぬける風が、あたかも外を吹き抜ける風と通い合うかのようなさわやかな気を漂わせて、新鮮な驚きをもって人々に受け入れられた。

自然の空間の中に身を置き、心を自由にそのうちに遊ばせるといった上野の制作態度は80年代から常に一貫した態度といってよいだろう。彼女にとっては布が作る形そのものはさして大きな問題ではない。自然から感じる様々な気分、それは時には安らぎであり、また時には畏れや驚きであったりする、目に見えないものを、作品をつくることによって表すのである。

80年代の後半から、竹の枝をシルクオーガンジーと組み合わせた作品が生まれているが、それも竹藪の側に住まうようになったせいだという。風に吹かれてゆったりと身をゆらせる竹の姿、葉のすれあうざわめき、春には筍が頭をもたげたかと思うと、見る間に成長して、大きくなって若竹になっていく竹の生命力の強さ、その後に続く落ち葉のゆったりとした、又時にはくるくると旋回しながら舞い落ちる様など、上野は竹藪を楽しむというか、心を自由に竹藪と通わせ、そのうちに解き放っていたのであろう。その後、楮、木、土などを素材とした作品に転じたのも、竹を育む大地の力、その神秘にうたれたからであろう。

上野真知子は作品の素材として様々なものを用いるが、決して自らの意に従わせるといった用い方はしない。素材それぞれの特性や性質をいかしながら用いるのである。それは、彼女の表現同様、こだわりのない、自由な心の賜であると言えよう。そうした心の故にこそ、上野真知子は自然のどんなひそやかな声も聞き、どんな僅かな表情の変化をも見逃すことはないのだと思う。

京都国立近代美術館長
内山武夫

From the early 1980s, Machiko Agano, who studied traditional weaving at the Kyoto City University of Arts, began exhibiting installations using fine and translucent fabrics such as silk organza. These installations were selected for exhibition at the 1992 Biennale Internationale de la Tapisserie, Lausanne, Switzerland.

At the Biennale, she was given a large exhibition space spreading over three floors. She filled the hall with a mass of fabrics hung in cascading zigzagging folds flowing through the space like liquid. The draughts blowing through the fabric were refreshingly reminiscent of the breezes outside the space. Agano's audience was again very receptive to her work.

Since the 1980s, she has maintained a creative attitude that places her within nature and allows her creativity freedom to roam there.

For her, the actual format from which the fabric is made is not important. The various moods sensed from nature are sometimes peaceful, sometimes amazing.

In her creations she expresses the inexpressible, she expresses what cannot be seen.

She has been combining bamboo and silk organza in her work since the late 1980s, apparently inspired by a bamboo grove next to her home. The form of a bamboo sculpture sways gently in the breeze with the murmur like that of rustling leaves. In spring, bamboo shoots appear in the grove and seem to grow visibly. The fluttering leaves seem to relate almost casually to the life force of two large bamboos. In this way, she allows her heart to enter the bamboo grove and to move freely within it.

Since then, moved by the mystery of the power of the earth that gives life to the bamboo, the materials for her work have moved on – to camellias, trees and earth.

Machiko Agano uses various materials for her work, but she never forces them to obey her intentions. She uses the characteristics and inherent nature of each material. They can be described as the fruits of her free heart. Because of her sensitivity to nature, Machiko Agano accepts its whispering voices and does not fail to notice their subtle changes of expression.

Takeo Uchiyama
Director, The National Museum of Modern Art, Kyoto, Japan

Machiko Agano: In Concert with the Wind

上野真知子 ― 風との共演

Untitled
1987
installation
silk organza, bamboo

上野真知子が麗らかな幕に包まれてアート界に現れた。数多い作家陣の中で、自身の精神性を巧みに表現できる作家がいるとすれば上野真知子がそれに当たる。というのも彼女が常に自身のことを深く理解していたからだろう。猫に魅了された子供の頃のこと、日本を拠点に世界中を巡る旅人であること、仏教の信奉者であり、またコンテンポラリーアートの使命を負った者として。上野は言うまでもなく、伝統的な意味でのテキスタイルを学んだ。そして京都市立芸術大学にて大学院を修了後、学生時代をすばやく置き去って作家となったのである。

風は止んでいるときでも、自然の中で最も不思議な要素の一つだ。上野の作品は風から生まれる。1983年の上野がまだ二十代の頃に、スイス、ローザンヌで行われた第11回国際タペストリービエンナーレに出展したインスタレーション作品をきっかけに、彼女は国際的なファイバーアート界に躍り出た。上野の作品は大きいスペースを要した。シルクオーガンジーによるパネルは、繊細な木の棒の間から吊るされ、ギャラリーで生じる風に応じて微妙な動きを見せた。その風はギャラリーの中を歩く人々によって生じたりし、戸の開閉によるものや、美術館の換気扇のスイッチが入っているかどうかによって微妙に異なった。半透明のシルクから見える光。透明な空気が作品に浸透してしまっているようかのようだった。自然が作品と一体化していた。こうしてアートにおいて欠くことのできない要素だったはずの「技巧」は上野の作品においては全く席を外すことになった。

Machiko Agano came into this world wrapped in a shroud of serenity. If ever there was an artist whose work reveals her spiritual being, it is Machiko Agano. For this is an artist who always knew who she was – a child mesmerized by cats, a traveler at home in the international world, a follower of Buddhism, disciple of contemporary art. Certainly she studied textiles in a traditional way, completing a post-graduate course at Kyoto University of the Arts. But quickly, she finished her studies, put school behind her, and became an artist.

The wind, even when quiet, is the most mysterious of all natural forces. Machiko Agano makes art born of the wind. In 1983, while still in her twenties, she broke into the international fiber world with an installation in the 11th International Biennial of Tapestry in Lausanne, Switzerland. Her art commanded a large gallery. Silk organza panels, hung between delicate wooden rods, floated in the breeze as people walked by, as doors opened and closed, as the museum's ventilation system switched off and on. Light filtered through the diaphanous silk. Transparent air rested at the soul of the work. It was as if nature itself had become a part of the exhibition. Artifice, that endless companion to art, had taken a vacation.

Untitled
1982
silk organza
seven pieces:
8 x 3 x 3ft (2.5 x 1 x 1m)

15

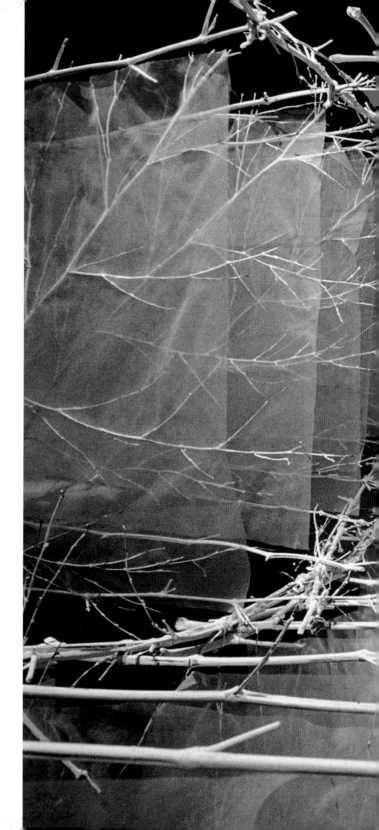

*We Japanese say that there
is something mysterious –
an invisible force –
in nature. I feel this is so.*

*I try to show this invisible,
all-encompassing force
through my work.*

Untitled (detail)
1991
silk organza,
bamboo acrylic resin
10 x 10 x 18ft (3 x 3 x 5.5m)

left:

Untitled
(detail, see also p21)
1988
silk organza,
bamboo acrylic resin
3 x 3 x 18ft (1 x 1 x 5.5m)

A few years later the silk organza panels shed their bamboo harness in her spectacular 1987 exhibition at Gallery Maronie in Kyoto. Stretching, reaching, the transparent cloth appeared to have been tossed into space by the wind, driven from a far gallery corner into the light (p12). Here was art closer to theater, to performance, to music, than to the static visual arts. Here was a new artist at the forefront of a new contemporary Japanese fiber movement.

There are places in the world, such as the Great Plains of North America with its prevailing westerlies, or the Gobi Desert of Inner Mongolia with its shifting yellow sands, where the wind blows endlessly. The inhabitants of those vast lands only remember the wind in moments of stillness.

For to know the wind is to live with its absence as well as its presence. Over the years Agano's work has engaged the wind in all its manifestations: movement and stillness, energy and repose.

In 1987 Agano moved from her home at the heart of Kyoto to an area west of the city famous for bamboo. She began to walk inthe bamboo forest, discovering its beauty, seeking to know its temperament. Agano installed her art in the park near her home and saw how nature enveloped, altered, and clarified her already simple structures (pp18, 21). To her it "looked like a bird or cloth that had been washed." She moved the installation into the Art Gallery of Western Australia in Perth and found "the same work looked as if it were different work in the different situation."

Untitled

1991

pulp, kozo, soil, sisal,

bamboo, wood

4 x 3 x 3ft (125 x 90 x 90cm)

数年後、このシルクオーガンジーを用いた作品から竹の引き具は取り除かれ、1987年の京都市内にあるギャラリーマロニエにて発表された息を呑むような作品へと変化を遂げた。半透明の布は伸びたり広がったりしながら、微かな風によってギャラリーの一角から、光の当たる場所へと運ばれていくようだった。静的なアートの展示空間というよりは、むしろ劇場でのパフォーマンス及び音楽という感じがした。新しい作家による、新しい日本のファイバーアートの始まりだった。

ところで世界には、風によってその様子を絶え間なく変え続けている場所がある。例えば、北アメリカにあるグレートプレーンズでは西よりの風が常に吹きながら地形を少しずつ変えている。また、内モンゴルのゴビ砂漠でも風によって動く黄色い砂がその様相を変え続けている。これらの広大で静かな土地の住人達には風の動きのみがその静けさの中で記憶に刻まれる。風を知るためには風が止まっている時だけでなく、吹いているときも経験しなくてはならない。何年にも渡り、上野の作品は風の特徴―動き、静止、力そして休息―と密接な関係を築いてきた。

1987年に上野は、住み慣れた京都の中心部から竹で有名な西部の街に引っ越した。それから彼女は竹薮を頻繁に歩くようになり、その美しさと激しさを新たに発見したのである。そして彼女は、作品を自宅近くにある公園に設置することにより、作品がどのように自然を包みこみ、様子を変え、そして彼女の作品の特徴だったシンプルな形をより明確な形で表すかを再確認した。上野にとってそれは「まるで鳥か、洗いざらしの布」のように見えた。彼女は同じ作品を西オーストラリアの都市、パースにある、Art Gallery of Western Australia にて発表した。上野は「同じ作品を、異なる環境に設置することによって全く新しい作品として見えた。」と述べている。

Untitled (detail)
1988
silk organza,
bamboo acrylic resin
3 x 3 x 18ft (1 x 1 x 5.5m)

"In the 1992 Lausanne Biennial, Agano moved indoors with a monumental structure that visually dominated the grand staircase of the museum. This time the wind was present in the large gestures of the bamboo, brought to life in the natural darkness of the interior by dramatic gallery lighting that penetrated and reflected off the contained silk organza. It was as if a fierce gale had swept into the building."

Untitled
1992
silk organza,
bamboo, acrylic resin

同年再びローザンヌビエンナーレに招かれた上野は、風によってインスパイアされた作品を発表した。間もなくして、パースのギャラリーで展示した作品と似た作品を京都のギャラリーマロニエにて発表した。竹による骨組みのなかに、オーガンジーを張ったその作品は、musee cantonal des beaux-arts の庭にも展示された。シルクオーガンジーの動きは竹の骨組みによって制限されたものの、代わりに太陽と雲がインスタレーションに加わったことによって空間に影が生まれ、風が全体に動きを与えた。上野は1992年のローザンヌビエンナーレより展示場所を屋外から屋内へと移した。そのときの彼女の記念碑的作品は会場の階段を飾った。風の動きは、薄暗いギャラリーの中で竹の巨大な骨組みに現れた。そして、それらを覆うシルクオーガンジーを照らす劇的な照明によって作品はその生命を得た。それはあたかも激しい風が建物の中に吹き込んだかのようだった。

上野は間もなくして、その半透明で微かに光るシルクの布から離れる。彼女の日ごろからの竹薮での精神的な対話が、彼女自身の関心をもっと「地」に近づけたのだ。それでは一体、上野はどのようにして地面の要素を作品の中で表現したのか？彼女は竹の繊維を用いて紙を作り、それに楮、アバカ、サイザル麻、そしてホコリを混ぜたものを加えて形を作るというプロセスに傾倒していった。それを円形のディスク状に象ったもの（一度に100個）をブロック上にして展示したのである。作品を「反復させる」ことによって作家のコンセプトは広がりを見せ、やがて一つの形へと繋がっていったのである。それに続いて上野は、地面のかけらを、一メートル状の鉄の棒を60本束ねることによって表現し、60本の束を一つのグループとして床面から一メートル上に、一直線に間隔を置かずに並べた。その直線は果てしなく延びていく様であり、事実そういう展示の仕方もオランダ、アメリカ、デンマーク、そしてオーストラリアにて行われた。恐らく、観客はこのドラマティックな光に照らし出された展示スペースに入ると同時に「あぁ、この作家は空と地面を同時に一つの空間へと持ち込んだのか。」という印象を受けたのだろう。

Untitled

1989

silk organza, bamboo, acrylic, resin

10 x 10 x 20ft (3 x 3 x 6m)

That same year she was again invited to participate in the Lausanne Biennial and once more the artist submitted art fashioned from the wind. Similar to the work shown in Perth and shortly after in Gallery Maronie in Kyoto, she stretched the organza within a rigid bamboo structure. Installed in the garden of the Musee Cantonal des Beaux-arts, the movement of the silk organza was arrested by the bamboo. Instead, the sun and clouds moved over and through the installation and the wind made its presence known in shifting shadows. Then, in the 1992 Lausanne Biennial, Agano moved back indoors with a monumental structure that visually dominated the grand staircase of the museum. This time the wind was present in the large gestures of the bamboo, brought to life in the natural darkness of the interior by dramatic gallery lighting that penetrated and reflected off the contained silk organza. It was as if a fierce gale had swept into the building.

Soon after, Agano set aside the transparent, shimmering silk cloth. Her regular forays into the bamboo forest had brought her closer to the earth. But how could she create the essence of earth? The artist began to integrate thin bamboo twigs into handmade paper, combining them with kozo, a member of the mulberry family; abaca, a relative of the banana plant; sisal; and dirt. Calling upon repetition to expand and compound her idea, she formed the ooze into round discs – hundreds at a time – to use as building blocks for installations Subsequently, she would string her chips of earth on meter-long iron rods, sixty to a rod. The artist mounted the rods close together in a line, one meter off the ground. The line could stretch endlessly, and it did, in the Netherlands, the USA, Denmark, and Australia. Dramatically lit, the viewer entered the exhibition space knowing that somehow this artist had brought earth and sky together.

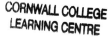

"I am attracted by the mysterious shapes of nature: patterns made by the wind on desert sands; shapes of eroded rocks on coastal shores; clouds driven across the autumn sky.

This is my art: the exploration and expression of the fundamentals of nature."

Untitled 2000
fishing line, stainless wire, sea weed paper
11 x 16 x 44 ft (8.5 x 5 x 14m)
Collection of Rias Ark Museum of Art, Japan

Untitled
1994
pulp, kozo, soil, bamboo, manila hemp
19in x 32ft x 3ft (0.5 x 10 x 1m)
collection of The Art Gallery of
Western Australia

right:
Untitled
1993
pulp, kozo, soil, sisal, bamboo,
manila hemp
17in x 12ft x 3ft (0.5 x 3.8 x 1m)

上野は意識的に、風と地面という要素を作品の課題として選んだのだろうか？ 恐らく答えはノーである。彼女が自然から得た素材と自身の抽象的なアイデア (光と影、動きと空間、存在と空虚さ) を使って試行錯誤することを選んだ結果なのである。

上野真知子の作品は彼女の自然に対する情熱を超えて日本の文化背景にも深く根ざしている。例えば、**飾り**。これは装飾を施すことと陳列することを表し、何世紀にも渡って姿かたちを変えながらも、常に文化の中に登場する日本古来のコンセプトである。古くから日本人は「普通の日」と「そうでない日」を祝いの儀式と祝宴を設けることによって変化をつけていた。特別な日に行事が行われる空間は、習慣としてその感謝の気持ちを表すために装飾によって変化が施されたのである。実際の**飾り**は、歌舞伎の装飾品、巨匠による浮世絵の世界や伝統的な祭りなどに見られる、目を見張るような装飾を指す。一見これらは、現代のファイバーアート作品からはかけ離れているようにも見える。しかし空っぽの空間そのものを、特別で不思議な世界 (＝展示会場) として変化させる、というのは上野真知子が常に作品の中で行っていることではないだろうか。

Did Agano consciously choose wind and earth as her subject? Probably not. Instead she chose to work abstractly with light and shadow, with movement in space, with being and nothingness, with abstract ideas played out with materials from the natural world.

Machiko Agano's art is deeply rooted in the history of Japanese culture in ways beyond her passion for nature. For example, *kazari*, which translates as 'decoration and display,' is an ancient concept that appears and reappears in various guises over the centuries. The Japanese differentiate between ordinary days and extraordinary days set aside for feasts and celebrations.

Kazari, an allay of ritual and pleasure, prescribes the transformation of the place or space where happenings take place on extraordinary days. In reality, *kazari* is the embellishment of the marvelous, be it *kabuki*, the courtesan's Floating World, or traditional festivals. On the surface, this might seem quite removed from the work of a contemporary Japanese artist working in fiber. Yet to take an empty exhibition space, itself the venue for something extraordinary, and to turn it into a magical world is exactly what Machiko Agano does.

Untitled
1996
installation
fishing line, stainless wire

this page:
Untitled
1991
pulp, kozo, soil, sisal, bamboo, wood
fourteen pieces, overall dimensions:
10 x 71 x 71in (25 x 185 x 185cm)

far right:
Untitled (detail)
1995
pulp, kozo, soil, sisal, bamboo, manila
hemp, expanded polystyrene
fourteen pieces, overall dimensions:
4 x 13 x 8in (110 x 35 x 20cm)

それだけでなく、**飾り**の美学は本質的な部分において上野真知子の芸術と一致する。多摩美術大学学長、東京大学名誉教授である、辻惟雄氏は**飾り**の権威として知られている。同氏は**飾り**を幻想、驚嘆、非対称性、誇張、様式化、即効性、遊び心、奇抜さと動きであると定義している。装飾という点において、上野の作品は一致しないようにも見える。それは彼女による装飾が、画家が画面を塗り陶芸家が技巧を施すそれとは異なるからだ。上野の作品において、装飾とは光と共演するための素材選びとそれに伴う触感の豊富さを指す。彼女のインスタレーションを支配する、鮮やかに揺れて、ひらひらしながらかすかに光る要素は卓越である。上野の計算しつくされた照明と作品の配置 (陳列) と、**飾り**のもう一つ別な意味である非対称性はインスタレーションの中で繰り返され、様式化、即効性、遊び心そして奇抜さによって誇張される。そしてそれら全てが「風による動き」によって生命を得るのである。上野の作品は形と触感、光と空間という要素の相互作用の中で、あらゆる時代の**飾り**の定義を含みながら、二十世紀と二十一世紀のはじめの新しい**飾り**のあり方をも例示している。

更に、2001 年に上野は英国においてブライトンフェスティバル関連のイベントとして、旧聖トリニティ教会で個展の依頼を受けた。彼女はその会場となった古い教会を予め訪れ、その不思議な空間に大変魅力を感じたという。上野は一旦帰国すると、太い編み棒を用いて編み始めた。1996 年より、シンプルなガーターステッチから去り、編むことによって作品を構成するようになっていた。上野は形の無い、ステンレスの細い糸とナイロンの釣り糸によって編んだ網状のものに楮を使って形にした。それらを製作過程の途中でイギリスへ一先ず送り、会場である、ブライトンの教会で他の要素 (光、空気、劇的な空間の雰囲気そのもの) を作品に取り入れながら完成させた。

The aesthetic system embedded in *kazari* seem equally fundamental to Machiko Agano's art. Nobuo Tsujii, President of Tama Art University and Professor Emeritus of the University of Tokyo and a leading scholar of *kazari*, defines it to include fantasy, surprise, asymmetry, exaggeration, stylization, improvisation, playfulness, eccentricity, and movement. Whereas Agano's work seems to deny decoration, it doesn't. Instead of occupying the surface as in painting or pottery embellishment, Agano's decoration is embedded in the textures she creates and in her choice of materials to play with light. Try to imagine a more glorious decoration than the flickering and glowing, dancing and gleaming, sparkling and shimmering, animated light that inhabits an Agano installation. Both her carefully-planned lighting and her placement of art within space – that is, display, the other half of *kazari* – are asymmetrical, exaggerated through repetition, stylized, improvised, playful, eccentric, and given life by movement. Agano's work exemplifies a new transformation of *kazari* in the late twentieth and early twenty-first century as it embodies all of the age old elements of *kazari* in its interplay with form and texture, with light and space.

To illustrate: in 2001 Machiko Agano was invited to create an exhibition in the former Holy Trinity Church as part of the Brighton Festival in England (p37). She visited the space, moved by its sense of both ancientness and mystery. Then she went home and began to knit – large needles, a simple garter stitch – in having switched to knitting in 1996 as a way to create structure. She transformed her formless mass of knitted stainless steel filament and nylon fishing line into a solidified configuration with *kozo* pulp, a type of Japanese handmade paper. Half finished, she shipped the work to England to be joined with its other components, that is, light, air, and the atmosphere of the lovely old building.

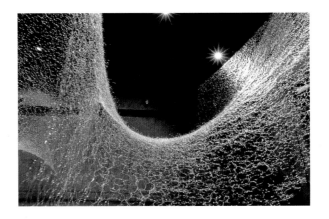

right:
Untitled 2001
fishing line, stainless wire, kozo
13 x 19 x 48ft (4 x 6 x 15m)
commissioned by Brighton Festival
and Surrey Institute

above:
Untitled
1997
fishing line, stainless wire
13 x 19 x 26ft (4 x 6 x 8m)

Untitled
2001
fishing line, stainless wire, kozo
13 x 19 x 48ft (4 x 6 x 15m)

この作品は巨大で多くの空間を占めていたため、観客は脇から眺めるというよりも、自然にインスタレーションそのものの中に入っていった。他の上野の作品からも伺えるように、この作品においても光が作品に命を吹き込む要素となっていた。ぼうっと空間に浮かぶ網の持つ触感と光は、教会の中にそれ自体の影を繰り返し映し出した。それはまるで魔法にかけられたかのようだった。スチールはほのかに光を放ち、殆ど見えないナイロンの糸は時折きらきらと光っていた。それは息を呑むほど美しく、まるで竹薮をあるいているかの様な気分になり、時が止まってしまったかのようだった。観客は会場に入るために建物の外に列を作っていた。上野の作品は決して自然と張り合おうとするのでは無く、自然を変わらない形で留め新たに、「作品」として表現するのである。

日本の現代ファイバーアーティストに共通のコンセプトとして、その空間の扱い方が挙げられる。彼らにとって、空間は作品と同等の存在感を持つ重要な素材の一つなのだ。これは海外のファイバーアーティストと著しく異なる。西洋の作家達の中では唯一、アメリカ人作家のアンハミルトンがこのコンセプトを表現し得るのではないだろうか。

上野真知子は**飾り**を現代に再び蘇らせながら、アートと自然の類まれなハーモニーを生み出す。彼女は国際的なアート界に存在していながらも、こうして極めて日本的な感性を持つめずらしい作家である。上野の狙いは自然についての作品を作るのではなく、観客に彼女のアートを通して自然の不思議さに触れてもらうのが目的である。これが本能的に、自分がアートに何を求めるべきかを理解して風と共に歩むことを選んだ作家の注目すべき点だと言えるだろう。

ノースダコタ美術館　館長
ローレル　リューター

Because this nameless work was huge, occupying a vast space, the viewer entered into it rather than looked on from the sideline. Like all of Agano's installations, the lighting was charged to bring the work to life, and, as always, it did. Agano's ghostlike web of texture and light cast a spell upon the space, filling it with repeating shadows of itself. The steel gleamed and the often invisible nylon line glistened. It was breathtakingly beautiful, akin to walking in her magical bamboo forest. Stillness inhabited the space. Crowds waited in line to enter. Once again this artist succeeded in capturing nature, not emulating it.

The concept that the space itself must be integrated into the work of art as an equal player is what sets contemporary Japanese fiber artists apart from their peers around the world. One could argue that only the American Ann Hamilton consistently achieves this goal among all of the western artists allied with the fiber field.

Machiko Agano, while redefining *kazari* for the contemporary world, merges art and nature into an uncommon harmony that is deeply Japanese while being quite at home in the international art world. She set out not to make art about nature, but to enter into the mystery of nature through her art. She wished the viewer to be enveloped by the atmosphere that inhabits her work, and she succeeds. What a remarkable achievement from one who intuitively understood from the onset what she could ask of her art, from one who chose to keep company with the wind.

Laurel Reuter
Director
North Dakota Museum of Art

untitled
1997
fishing line, stainless wire, silk
13 x 19 x 11ft (4m x 6m x 3.5m)

Biography

Born

1953   Kobe, Japan

Education and Awards

1979   Completed the Post Graduate Course of Kyoto University of Arts, Kyoto

1989   9th Imadate Exhibition of Contemporary Paper Art, Outstanding Award

1990   1st Contemporary Crafts Exhibition by Selected Artists, Excellence Award

1992   2nd Contemporary Crafts Exhibition by Selected Artists, Excellence Award

1993   12th Imadate Exhibition of Contemporary Paper Art, Japan Paper Academy Award

Profressional

Professor, Textile Department, Kyoto Seika University

Solo Exhibitions

1978, 80   Gallery Iteza, Kyoto

1982, 83, 84   Utsubo Gallery, Osaka

1984, 86   Esses Gallery, Tokyo

1986   Lyran's Gate, Kobe

1987, 89, 93, 97   Gallery Maronie, Kyoto

1987, 89   Shoe Gallery, Ohta, Ashiya

1988, 91, 96, 99   Gallery Gallery, Kyoto

1991   Kyoto Municipal Shijo Gallery, Kyoto

2001   Fabrica Gallery, Brighton, England

Selected Group Exhbitions

1979	'Contemporary Arts & Crafts,' Gunma Prefectural Museum of Modern Art, Gunma
1983, 87, 92	'International Biennial of Tapestry,' Musée Cantonal de Beaux Arts, Lausanne, Switzerland
1984	'4th Hara Annual,' Hara Museum of Modern Art, Tokyo
	'Running Art '84,' Shiga, Takamatsu, Osaka, Japan
1985	'Art Now '85,' Hyogo Prefectural Museum of Modern Art, Hyogo, Japan
1986	'Contemporary Art Exhibition,' Taipei Fine Art Museum, Taipei
1988	'Fibres et Fils,' Musée d'art et d' Histoire, Belfort, France
1988, 89	'1st, 4th Perth International Crafts Triennial,' The Art Gallery of Western Australia, Perth
1988, 90, 93, 95	'9th, 10th, 12th, 14th Imadate Exhibition of Contemporary Paper Art,' Fukui, Japan
1990	'Cross Threads' Bradford, UK
1990, 92	'1st, 2nd Contemporary Crafts Exhibition by Selected Artists,' Kyoto
1991	'Restless Shadows'' (tour UK)
1991, 98, 00	'Art Exhibition of Selected Artists,' Kyoto Municipal Museum
1993	'Fascinate Textiles,' Museum Van Bommel – Van Dam, Venlo, The Netherlands
	'Shiga Annual '93,' The Museum of Modern Art, Shiga, Japan
1994	'Light and Shadow – Japanese Artists in Space,' North Dakota Musuem of Fine Art, USA
	'Asian Heart and Form,' NTT Credo Hall, Hiroshima
1995	'Contemporary Crafts in Kyoto,' The Museum of Kyoto
1996	'CONTAINER '96 – Art Across Oceans,' Copenhagen, Denmark
	'Japanese Dyeing Weaving Textile,' Meguro Museum of Fine Art, Tokyo

Selected Group Exhbitions continued

1998	'IMAGINATIONS '98', Contemporary Japanese Textile Exhibition, Gastuiskapel, Belgium
	'Japanese Textile Miniatures Folding,' Canberra Museum and Gallery, Australia (tour)
1998, 00	'Dyeing Seiryu Ten,' Kyoto Municipal Museum, Meguro Museum of Fine Art, Tokyo
1999	'International Textile Competition '99 Kyoto,' The Museum of Kyoto
	'Dyeing Weaving Crafts of Silk,' Kiryu Municipal Hall, Japan
2000	'The Seaweed's Paper & Four Artists,' Rias Ark Museum of Art, Miyagi, Japan
	'Folding,' The Museum of Arts and Crafts Itami, Hyogo, Japan
2001	'Textural Space' – Contemporary Japanese Textile Art, Foyer Gallery, Farnham, UK (tour)
	'Miniatures from Textural Space,' Beardsmore Gallery, London
2002	'PAPER WORKS 2002 INO,' Kochi, Japan
	'Light, Thread, Shadow '– Japanese and Bulgarian Contemporary Textile Art, Bulgaria (tour)

Work in Public Collections

Mary Toms – Pierre Pauli Foundation, Lausanne, Switzerland

Kyoto Prefecture, Japan

The National Museum of Art, Osaka, Japan

The Art Gallery of Western Australia

The Museum of Modern Art, Gunma, Japan

Rias Ark Museum of Art, Miyagi, Japan